Meet The Helicopters

Karin and Dan Garblik

Illustrations by TooDoo
http://too-doo-blog.tumblr.com

For Caden and Decker

Thank you for letting us hover over you.

We love you.

Heck yeah, meet the Helicopter Family!
There is Helicopter Mommy,
There is Helicopter Daddy,
And then there is Dax, the Baby!

They wait in line for pricey ice cream cones,
and at night they bingewatch Game of Thrones.

They jam to Drake and live by the Bay.
So... they seem normal in *almost* every way...

Pretty cool, right?!
But these parents didn't always have the gift of flight...

...they used to be discrete. Like everyone else you meet,
gravity kept their feet firmly on the street.

Until the moment Baby Dax was born
and propellers sprouted from their heads like horns.

Mommy looked in Dax's big, shiny eyes
and her heart swelled up with love and pride;
but then she nervously asked if his skin was dry,
and her propellers expanded three feet wide.

11

With Dax to dote on, a new joy they discovered
was instead of walking to places, they now hovered.

Helicopter parents have such a blast carrying their children to a higher class.

Flying up high away from the sleazes that could give Dax diseases...

Floating above their Croatian Au Pair
makes it easy to see what she even does down there.

CELL PHONE CAMERA

APP-ENABLED SECURITY CAMERA

ZAP

They enrolled Dax in transcendental meditation;
apparently, it helps with preschool applications.

Dax drinks manually expressed, pour-over breast milk.

Prepared from eight feet high, at just the right tilt.

I just wish doctors would quantify his smile,
Because it'd def be 99th percentile.

17

At night, Dax needs a bath and then a fugue from Bach.
Otherwise, he won't be the happiest baby on the block.

Before getting his butt smeared with Aquaphor,
Dax reads a mindful book about endangered albacores.

Then artisanal lotion to prevent eczema,
while Mommy books his monthly baby enema...

Okay, it gets tiring to hover all the time.

It takes three freakin' hours for Dax's bedtime!

It may seem the Helicopters live the dream,
but other people think they can be extreme.

Maybe because they fuss and panic
if their baby food isn't organic.

Many other parents watch over their children, morphing to bring the family fulfillment.

Like, there's the Tiger Family living in Chinatown…

... Or the Molebergs, who built a bunker underground.

One day, they visit their laid-back friends, The Jellies, and discuss how they keep their kids healthy.

We just let Sojourner go with the flow;
Why do you hover? Where could Dax go?

But if we didn't cling from above,
how would Dax know that he's loved?

Could you imagine if we didn't pay attention?
Who would massage away his hypertension?

A ball slips and smacks Dax in the face.
Mommy flies to help, but Mrs. Jelly holds her in place.

They all stare at Dax, whose face was frozen.

29

But just before Mommy escapes from Mrs. Jelly's squeeze...

...and also a little fart.

...Dax scrunches up and lets out a huge sneeze!

And before Mommy and Daddy could zoom to hold him,
Dax's smile cracks, followed by laughs so emboldened.
Such laughter, such cheer!
Dax starts grinning from ear to ear!

Giggling, Dax keeps playing and throws the ball high,
they've never seen him so happy – they both nearly cry.

Who knew a little spontaneity
could relieve such anxiety?

Since then, Mommy and Daddy are often astounded
at how good it feels to stay a little grounded.

And all thanks to that fateful sneeze,
They learned it's sometimes good to let
Dax drift in the breeze.

We have to give Dax freedom
to reach for the sky!

Still though, we stay close...
to shoo away flies.

11961521R00022

Made in the USA
San Bernardino, CA
12 December 2018